Hold 'em Poker

By
David Sklansky

A product of Two Plus Two Publishing

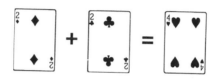

1997 EDITION

FIFTH PRINTING
February 2004

Printing and Binding
Creel Printing Co.
Las Vegas, Nevada

Printed in the United States of America

Hold 'em POKER
COPYRIGHT © 1976, 1989, 1996, 2000 David Sklansky

For information contact: **Two Plus Two Publishing**
226 Garfield Dr.
Henderson NV 89014
(702) 896-1326

ISBN: 1-880685-08-6

To My Son Matty

Original Publisher's Forward

For quite a while, one of our most frequent requests at Gambler's Book Club was for a book on Texas hold 'em. Until now we could not fulfill this request for the simple reason that no such book existed. We felt that this situation had to be remedied as the game was rapidly sweeping the country. We therefore contacted David Sklansky to write the first book on hold 'em ever. What resulted was not merely the first hold 'em book, but also the first (we think) definitive work on any poker game, unlike any previous book on gambling.

David Sklansky is a professional gambler. He plays poker and blackjack for a living and has no other means of support. If he doesn't win, he doesn't eat. Moreover, he gambles almost exclusively in Las Vegas against the toughest competition in the world. He plays in games ranging in stakes from $10-$20 to $50-$100 to no-limit. The number of Vegas professionals with similar success can be counted on the fingers of one hand. However, what makes David Sklansky unique is that he is also a brilliant mathematician. Originally an actuary, and a much sought after math tutor, Sklansky became intrigued with the idea of gambling for a living. His teaching background combined with his gambling experience makes him uniquely qualified to write this book.

In the past, all books on poker have fallen into two general categories. Some have been written by expert "gamesmen" who have a good theoretical background, but very little practical experience. Their advice consists of rather vague generalities which are true enough, but lack the specific points one must understand in order to become an expert player. There are endless probability tables, but few hints as to how to use these tables under fire. Other authors claim to be professional gamblers with good advice on "hustling" the game. Their strategic advice is sadly lacking in accuracy.

This book is the first that *really* can show you how to be a great player. It is the first to explain those strategic concepts heretofore only understood by some professionals. While many of these concepts are based on mathematics, Sklansky dispenses with most of the theoretical work he did to arrive at them. He uses his teaching experience to put them across in as simple a way as can be expected. The persevering reader cannot help but become a first class hold 'em player if that is his desire.

Note to 1997 Edition

Since I first wrote this book some 20 years ago, the game of hold 'em poker has enjoyed an amazing surge in popularity. In 1976 there were only two games $10-$20 or higher in all of Nevada (and thus in all of the United States). Now there are hundreds of such games. (I'd like to think that this book had a little something to do with that.)

With all these new hold 'em players it is only natural that the caliber of play has improved. In spite of this, I was pleased to see when rereading this book after many years that almost all the principles in it still hold. However, a significant change in the game did need to be addressed. It has to do with the fact that bigger games usually have two "blinds" rather than the one blind assumed in earlier editions of this book. Since this second blind is usually twice the size of the first it has some affect on strategy and starting hands.[1] I have addressed these strategy changes when they come up both in footnotes and in the main body of the text where appropriate.

Throughout this book I indicate hands with letters and symbols. An "s" indicates a suited hand and an "x" indicates a small card. Note that a 10 is represented as "T." Also, if no "s" appears, then the hand is not suited.

For example if I say AT I mean an ace and a ten of two different suits. If I say ATs then the two cards are of the same suit. If I say A♠T♠ then I mean precisely the ace of spades and the ten of spades.

---

[1]Some readers will notice that the hand rankings in this book are slightly different from other hand rankings that I have published. This is because they were updated for this edition and are currently the most accurate rankings in print.

Part One

Getting Started

Getting Started

Introduction

Hold 'em poker is fast becoming one of the most popular poker games in America. However, there is virtually nothing in print at this writing that gives more than a cursory look at this game.[2] I intend to remedy that with this book. This is not simply an elementary introduction to the game. I believe that anyone who thoroughly understands everything in this book can become a top notch hold 'em player with a little experience. However, do not expect easy reading. Most people will find that they will have to read certain sections over two and three times before they can expect to fully understand the concepts contained in them. At the same time I will assume the reader has a prior knowledge of poker in general. Those readers who haven't played any kind of poker at all would be wise to pick up a book such as the *Fundamentals of Poker* by Mason Malmuth and Lynne Loomis before continuing with this book.

---

[2]This was in 1977. Now of course there is *Hold 'em Poker For Advanced Players* by myself and Mason Malmuth.

Dealing a Few Hands

At the beginning of each hand of hold 'em, the dealer starting at his left, deals around until each player has two cards face down. The deal moves to the left after each hand. (In casino games there is a house dealer so a rotating "button" is put in front of a player to signify that he is the dealer for that hand, and thus gets cards last and acts last in each betting round.) There is one round of betting on these first two cards. The dealer now deals three consecutive cards face up in the middle of the table. These cards are called the "flop." They are community cards used in common by every player still in the hand. There is then a second round of betting. After that, a fourth card is dealt face up and a third round of betting occurs. A fifth and final card is then turned up and a last round of betting takes place. If there is more than one player left in the game at the end, the winner of the pot is the player with the best poker hand using the best five out of seven cards (the two in his hand and the five in the middle). Occasionally there is a split pot. Before defining the rules of play more explicitly I will give some examples of possible hands:

3

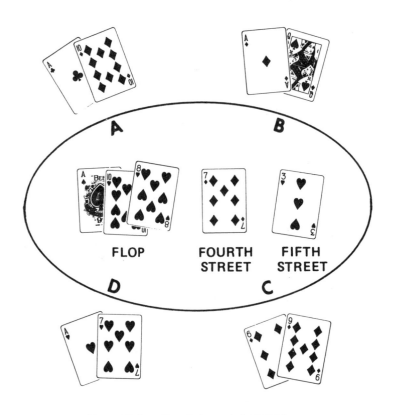

Player A's best five cards are A A 10 10 8
Player B's best five cards are A A Q 10 8
Player C's best five cards are 6 7 8 9 10
Player D's best five cards are A 10 8 7 3 All hearts

Therefore in this example, Player D has the best hand with an ace high flush. Notice he also has aces and sevens if he chooses to use a different combination of five cards. But, of course, he wouldn't do that and in this case he is lucky he made a flush on the last card since Player A has aces and tens and Player C has a straight. Here is another example:

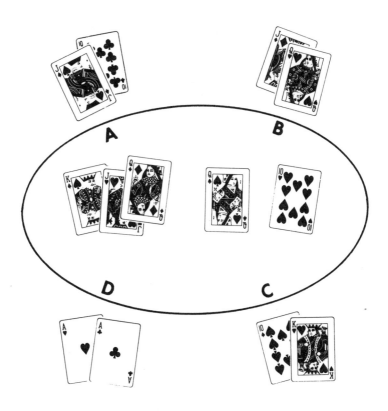

Player A has Q Q J J K
Player B has Q Q Q J J
Player C has K K Q Q J
Player D has A K Q J 10 - straight

In this case player B wins with a full house. Notice that both hole cards are not always used to make your best hand. It is possible to have the best hand even if you are using only one of your hole cards and your opponent is using both of his. However, if neither card in your hand is used that is called "playing the board" and in this case the most you can hope for is a split pot (if your opponent also plays the board). One last example:

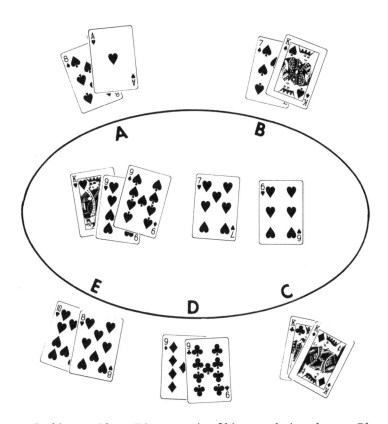

In this case Player B's two pair of kings and nines lose to Player A's ace-high heart flush. However, Player C beats that with kings full only to be beaten by Player D's four nines, and Player E's straight flush!

The reader should double check this last example. Figuring your best hand is not always as easy as it may appear. While I won't give any further examples, I urge the reader to deal out a few hundred hands himself until he can instantly recognize his best hand.

The Best Possible Hand

Another related concept is figuring the best possible hand that can be held, given the cards in the middle (also called the cards "on board"). The second best hand, third best, etc. can also be figured. An Example:

In this case the best possible hand anyone could hold would be three kings, followed by three queens, three eights, etc. The general rule is that there cannot be a full house or four-of-a-kind in the game without a pair on board. Also, there cannot be a flush or straight flush without at least three of a suit on board. Straights must be figured individually. In this example if the Q♦ was the J♦ instead, someone holding a T9 would have a straight.

A second example: The cards on board are:

In order, the best hands are:
> Four jacks if you held JJ.
> Four eights if you held 88.
> Aces full if you held AA.
> Jacks full of Aces if you held AJ.
> Jacks full of eights if you held J-anything.

Eights full of aces if you held A8.
Eights full of jacks if you held 8-anything.
A flush if you held two diamonds.
AAJJK if you held AK.
AAJJQ if you held AQ.
AAJJT if you held AT.
AAJJ9 if you held A9.
AAJJ8 if you held A7, A6, A5, A4, A3, or A2.
Kings over jacks if you held KK.

Let us notice something: One of the points of this exercise is to ascertain whether we, in fact, have the "nuts" (a lock). Sometimes, when it appears that a certain hand could conceivably beat us, one of our own cards might block this possibility. If the cards on board are KKJJ4 and we are holding KJ — nothing can beat us since we are blocking four-of-a-kind. If the board is 6♥8♥9♥K♦Q♦ we have the nuts with A♥7♥ since we block the straight flush.

A final example: The cards on board are:

You can't be beaten if you hold J♥9♥ or 9♥6♥. Your next best hole cards are 8♦8♠ followed by AA, TT, A8, T8, 87, 77, and then K♥-anything.

The reader should learn these concepts also by dealing out a few hundred hands and determining the nuts, the second nuts, etc. This is important because in hold 'em it is not that rare to get a hand that can't possibly lose and obviously, it is important to know when you have one.

Different Variations

Let us now look at the different variations in the betting rules of hold 'em poker. A well-known variation is "no-limit" (actually "table stakes"). This is the game that is played in the finals of the World Series of Poker every year at Binion's Horseshoe Casino in Las Vegas. However, no beginner should even consider playing it. It is not a friendly game. This book will concentrate on the "limit" variety of this game.

In all ensuing problems I will assume that the reader is playing in the $10-$20 hold 'em game at The Mirage in Las Vegas (unless otherwise noted). This will be done to simplify and standardize the examples to follow. These are the rules:

> There is no ante. However the player to the left of the dealer button must put in $5 and the player to his left must put in $10. These bets are called the "small blind" and the "big blind." The next player must either fold, call the $10 or raise to $20. From then on raises before the flop are in increments of $10. There is usually a maximum of four raises allowed. If no one raises the player who put in the big blind he is given the opportunity to raise himself. This feature is called a "live blind." The second round of betting (after the flop) is in units of $10 starting from the small blind, if he is still in, proceeding to the left. The player may check at this point, or bet $10. Check and raise is allowed. The betting on "fourth street" and "fifth street" (fourth and fifth cards on board) once again starts to the left of the button, this time in units of $20.

Make sure you understand all these rules in order to best follow later examples.

Most limit games have the same general structure as The Mirage $10-$20 game. In a few places check-and-raise is prohibited. Some games do not have a blind. However, in every game I have seen without a blind, it was mandatory to bet or get out on the first two cards. Checking was not allowed on this round. In some games there is a choice of how much to bet. None of these variations significantly change playing strategy however.

There are two appealing characteristics of hold 'em that exist for any variation. One is that you can play with far more players than the usual number of seven or eight, even up to twenty can play since the cards do not run out! No one has to sit out of hands when ten people come to your poker party if you play hold 'em. Secondly, since a player's folding does not change the flop a player can see what hand he would have made even if he is out of the hand. He thus has the dubious opportunity to second guess himself.

Incidentally, some readers may have noticed that there appears to be a big advantage for the dealer (and disadvantage for those in early position) since he gets to act last on all four betting rounds. To those of you that did notice, congratulations, you are already on the way to becoming an expert hold 'em player.

Part Two

Position

Position

Introduction

A player's position is more important in hold 'em than in any other poker game. Only draw poker is close. In both draw and hold 'em the dealer acts last and the man "under the gun" acts first on each betting round. (In some forms of draw poker, the opener, rather than the man under the gun, acts first after the draw, which somewhat diminishes the dealer's advantage.) However, hold 'em has *four* betting rounds as opposed to draw poker's two. This fact serves to compound the advantages of late position and the disadvantages of early position.

Some Considerations

Why are these considerations so important? Here is an analysis: First, take the play before the flop. If you call in early position, you are subjecting yourself to one or more raises behind you. The earlier your position the more risk you are taking. If you wouldn't have called if you *knew* there was a raise behind you, you have now been forced to put $20 in before the flop with a hand that doesn't justify it. If you fold without calling the raise, you have given up $10 without seeing a card. Also some hands are only worth playing if there are many other callers. In early position you are just guessing about how many people will play.

Other considerations involve the fact that if you are in early position or under the gun, you will remain there throughout the hand. Assume now that it is sometime after the flop. Once again, if you are in last position with only a fair-to-good hand, and the first player bets, there can be no raise behind you. Those players in middle position have no such comfort. If you have a "big hand" in this spot, your advantage in being last is even greater. This is best seen by comparing your situation with being first with a big hand. If you were first you might try to check and raise, but if it doesn't work you have lost a few bets from those that would have called you, and given a free card to those that wouldn't. Being last, you will always be able to bet even if you don't get the opportunity to raise. If you are in middle position with a big hand, you still have problems. If no one has yet bet and it is up to you, you must decide whether to risk "sandbagging." Also, if someone has bet in front of you, a raise will drive players out behind you. These extra bets lost really add up.

Even if the pot narrows down to two players, these positional considerations still apply, maybe more so. Suppose you are last to act and have a big hand. Once again if your opponent bets you can raise. If he doesn't bet, you do. If you are first with the same hand, you can only make two bets if a check-raise works. If it doesn't, you

13

have cost yourself a bet. If instead you come right out betting with this hand in first position, you lose a bet when a check raise would have worked, but he now just calls. If your hand is only mediocre, it is once again advantageous to be last. If you can't call a bet, you still may get a free card (which could wind up beating him) if he chose to check a hand which you know is better than yours. However, if you are first with this same hand, it is unlikely that he will still check after you check. Finally, even if your hand is somewhere in the middle (good, but not great) it is better to be last. While it is true that you will bet in either position, if he is first, and comes out betting, you will simply call him. If you were first in this spot, you would bet and he might raise. The importance of these extra bets that may be saved or gained by being in late position cannot be overemphasized. Never forget that in poker we are trying to win a lot of money — not a lot of pots.

It is true as some sharp readers may have realized, that occasionally it is an advantage to be in early position. Sometimes you want to drive players out to make your hand stand up. Only raising in early position will do this. Secondly, if you are first with "a lock" you may make three bets by betting and then reraising. However, these exceptions do little to change the general principle that it is better to be last. (This, of course, is even more true when the check and raise feature is not allowed.)

How then do we make use of this information? Later on in the Strategy chapter I will discuss situations after the flop where your position determines your action. However, the main point of this chapter is to show why you must take your position very much into account when you are deciding whether to play a specific hand or not. Any starting hand can become a winning hand when all the cards are out. However, some hands do so more than others. For this reason, the lesser hands can be played only in late position. Not simply because you are in little danger of a raise behind you before the flop, but also because of the bets that are gained (or saved) when you turn a hand in this position. Conversely, the opposite considerations apply in early position. Therefore. the earlier your position, the better your first two cards must be to play. But what are good starting hands?

Part Three

The First Two Cards

The First Two Cards

Introduction

On the following page appears my list of the seventy-two top starting hands in order from the best to the worst. It is *rarely* correct to play a hand *not* on this list. I have separated these hands into eight groups. While the rankings of the hands within each group are subject to debate, there is little question that cards in a higher ranked group are better than those in a lower group. To a large degree, all hands in a particular group should be played the same way before the flop. Thus, if in a certain situation it is correct to raise with AQ, it is correct to raise with KQ suited. If it is correct to fold two eights "wired," it is correct to fold AJ offsuit. More on this in the strategy chapter.

There are some points about these rankings that the reader should understand before studying the list.

1. I am assuming a full game of eight to eleven players and moderately tight play (an average of about four players staying for the flop). Certain hands change value if there are very many (or very few) opposing hands. Small pairs and straight flush cards go up in value with many players. High cards and high pairs go down.

2. These rankings do not reflect how one hand will do head-up against another. Two nines is ranked below AK, for instance, even though it is a small favorite in "one on one" play. Rather these rankings reflect which hands will win the most pots and more importantly the most money over a period of time in a full game.

3. The list would have to be substantially altered for *no limit* games.

Two aces are the best hand, period. They are a little stronger with only a few callers, but no hand will win more pots or more money no matter how many people are in the pot.
An analysis of some of these hands follows:

Hand Groups

Group 1	1. AA 2. KK 3. QQ 4. JJ 5. AKs	Group 2	6. TT 7. AQs 8. AJs 9. KQs 10. AK
Group 3	11. 99 12. JTs 13. QJs 14. KJs 15. ATs 16. AQ	Group 4	17. T9s 18. KQ 19. 88 20. QTs 21. 98s 22. J9s 23. AJ 24. KTs
Group 5	25. 77 26. 87s 27. Q9s 28. T8s 29. KJ 30. QJ 31. JT 32. 76s 33. 97s 34. Axs 35. 65s	Group 6	36. 66 37. AT 38. 55 39. 86s 40. KT 41. QT 42. 54s 43. K9s 44. J8s 45. 75s
Group 7	46. 44 52. 22 47. J9 53. Kxs 48. T9 54. T7s 49. 33 55. Q8s 50. 98 56. 53s 51. 64s 57. 43s	Group 8	58. 96s 66. 42s 59. 85s 67. 32s 60. J7s 68. 87 61. 74s 69. 76 62. A9 70. 65 63. Q9 71. 54 64. J8 72. K9 65. T8

Analysis of the Hand Groups

Any *suited* hand is ranked higher than the same unsuited cards for obvious reasons. However, the difference is not as great as most people think. A flush is only made 6 percent of the time with these hands.[3] Furthermore, even if you make your flush you may find yourself losing a big pot to a higher flush. For this reason a hand like a king and a smaller card of the same suit is ranked 53rd on the list. Similarly KQ *offsuit* is ranked above KTs. It is true, however, that as your cards get lower you are counting quite a bit on your flush chances when you are suited. Thus J9s is ranked well above J9.

The same principle applies to straight cards. When you don't have high cards, it is better that the ranks of the cards be right next to each other. For example, 87 makes a straight with JT9, T96, 965, and 654. An 86 uses both cards to make a straight only with T97, 975, and 754. However, if the cards are not middle sized, the numbers of straight combinations decreases and the aforementioned principles may not hold. Thus AK makes a straight one way while KJ does it two ways. Both 32 and 42 make straights two ways. The reader should reflect on these principles so that he can immediately see the number of combinations making straights using both cards for any hand. The answer will always be between zero and four.

AKs is usually slightly better than TT because it will win more money. TT can usually only win a big pot if a ten falls. If an ace or a king (or Q or J) falls, the tens have no betting power and may even have to get out (losing its opportunity to catch one of the two remaining tens). If only small cards come, the tens will very possibly either get no action or run into a hand that beats them.

---

[3]This figure assumes you stay in even when only one of your suit flops. In actual play you will make a flush less than 5 percent of the time since you will usually not stay to catch two "running" cards.

However, if an ace or king flops, an AK can get action from an ace or a king with a smaller kicker. The fact that TT will win many smaller pots as well as a few big ones however does justify its inclusion in the Group 2 category.

AQ is about as good as ATs because it is much better than AT offsuit. First of all, if an ace flops, you have a better kicker. More importantly, if a queen falls to an AQ, this is good unless a king also falls. However, if a ten falls to AT there must be no king, queen, or jack for the hand to be worth much. The chance of pairing the lower card, yet still not having the best hand, makes quite a difference in the two hands. This concept came up quite often in formulating the rankings.

AT is a dangerous hand. I hesitated to rank it even as highly as I did, especially for beginners. The reason for this is that you can get into a lot of trouble with this hand. If you make two aces only, you must know how to get away from it, if it doesn't figure to be the best hand. You would rather the flop make you two tens (if it is the top pair) than two aces. A straight would be best. However, you will make the best hand with these cards often enough that, with experience, you should usually play them — especially when they are suited.

Hands like JTs usually must make a straight, two pair, or possibly a full house to make any serious money. Even a flush with this hand is in jeopardy of losing to a higher flush. If you flop top pair, you may just get into more trouble especially if you lack experience in these situations. Those writers who have called this the best hand, even in full games, are out of their minds!

Any pair below nines is really looking to flop three-of-a-kind. Except for the occasional times when they make a straight, little pairs cannot win any kind of decent pot without making "trips." Therefore, this is the reason that all the very small pairs are ranked near each other.

In general then, I used six interrelated criteria in formulating these rankings:

1. What are the chances of making the best hand?

2. What are the chances of making a flush? (Are the cards suited?)

3. What are the chances of making a straight. (Are the cards close to each other and in the middle ranges?)

4. What are the chances of flopping top pair (or in the case of a pair in the hole, what are the chances that no overcard will fall)?

5. What are the chances of making a hand that figures to win a big pot (because the players will tend to make second best hands)?

6. What are the chances of making a hand that might well just lose money since *it* will be second best?

This last criteria is very important. It is the reason that hands like KJ and KT are ranked as low as they are even though they will make the best hand more often than some of the hands ranked above them. When they do make the best hand, they don't figure to get any action. If they do get action they are frequently beaten (if the game is tough).

Likewise many hands in the lower groups are ranked there because of the propensity to make hands that will only get you into trouble. The exception is small pairs where you either make trips or get out.

All in all, what we are considering are which hands have the best chance of flopping cards that will show the most profit. Which brings us to the next section.

Part Four

Flops You Want

Flops You Want

Introduction

Hold 'em is a unique game inasmuch as you are *not* always hoping to make your best possible hand. The reason for this is that you may not get any action with these hands. If you hold AK you certainly are not hoping for three aces to fall. Even stranger is the fact a lesser hand may have a greater chance of being the best hand than a better one. A typical example of this would be if you are holding AJ. In this case J32 would be a better flop than A32. In the latter case you may easily be beaten by AQ or AK, as well as a straight. In the former case you beat anyone else who has jacks and only have to worry about the small chance that someone holds a higher pair in the hole. Also, when A32 flops, it is much more conceivable that someone has aces-up than that someone has jacks-up in the first example. Besides having a better chance of having the best hand when J32 flops to AJ, you would also prefer this flop because it figures to be more profitable. In this case you can expect action from KJ, QJ, or JT. When A32 flops, you can expect action only from AT and you will be the one giving action to AQ or AK.

It is even possible that you would like to flop a lesser hand not because it has a better chance of being the best hand but because it has a better chance of *making* the best hand. If you hold

you would prefer the flop to be

24

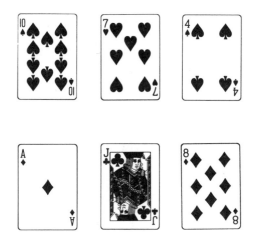

than

even though there is a better chance that two aces is the best hand with the second flop than two sevens is with the first flop. With the two sevens you are about even money to make aces-up, three sevens, or a nut flush. (You have two chances to catch any one of fourteen cards.) Add to this the fact that two sevens might be the best hand, and you now have a situation where you will wind up winning the pot more often starting with a *second pair* than with *top pair*. A similar but even more clear-cut example would be where you have

and the flop comes

I leave it to the reader to examine the possibilities of this example for himself.

This interesting aspect of hold 'em has led me to include a special chapter on the best flops for various hole cards. It is good preparation for the strategy section. Following is a table broken down into four columns. In the first column I list two hole cards. The second column shows examples of the best type of flops for these cards. The third column has examples of good flops. The fourth column gives examples of only fair and sometimes unplayable flops. I have not included every starting hand nor every example of the types of flops. What I have done is give enough illustrative examples so that the reader can discern the various criteria involved in making these evaluations. These criteria will be enumerated at the end of the chapter. I will also explain some of the more interesting entries in the table immediately following it.

Two Quick Points

I have assumed a typical fairly tight game with four to six players in the hand before the flop. With less players, you are more interested in having the best hand than in having a hand that will get action as you will get action anyway. For instance, if you flop a flush against one player, he won't be as much afraid of the three-flush on board against one opponent, and will give plenty of action with a top pair.

Secondly, I have assumed that you have little reason to believe that a very high pair in the hole is out against you. If there *were* some reason to believe this

would be a better flop to

than

Similarly:

would become a better flop to two jacks in the hole than

(If you are up against two aces you're dead, and if you are not, you'll get better action if the flop is J92 because kings or queens won't be afraid of the ace.)

Noting the exceptions let us proceed:

Hole Cards	Excellent Flops	Good Flops	Fair Flops
AA	KJ4 ATT 832	K♠J♠4♣ AJ6 T33	QQ3 9♣7♣6♣ KQJ
KK	Q84 KTT 832 AK5	Q♠T♠4♣ K32 T33 T♦8♣7♣	QQ3 A85 9♣7♣6♣ J♦T♦9♣
AK	A84 AK5 QJT	A66 AQT KK6	AQQ T83 A♥8♥5♥
A♦J♦	J♥8♦4♦ AJ5 KQT	T♦6♦2♦ AQT JJ6	AA6 A♥7♥6♣ KT9

Hole Cards	Excellent Flops	Good Flops	Fair Flops
K♦Q♦	K♥8♦4♦ AJT Q84 KQ3	KK7 QQ7 A♦6♦2♦ T♦6♦2♥	K77 T♥8♠3♦ AQT Q♥7♥3♥
JJ	AJ3 QQJ JTT	J92 JT9 852	A84 8♦6♠5♠ TT3
KJ	AQT KJ5	J84 QT3	K88 K♠T♣4♦
J♦T♦	987 JT4 T♣7♦8♦	J98 JJ3 Q♦3♦2♦	A♥9♦5♦ J84 9♥8♥7♥
A♦6♦	A68 A♥8♦5♦ Q66	Q♦8♦7♠ 652 T♦5♦2♦	A83 963 AA3
8♦7♦	872 654 Q♥6♦5♦	T87 986 T♦3♦2♦	543 832 8♥7♥6♥
Q♦8♦	Q84 Q♥7♦5♦ JT9	882 T♦3♦2♦ A88	Q63 863 T♦6♦3♥
66	AQ6 653 QQ6	633 6♥5♦4♦ 543	JJJ 732 975
7♦5♦	864 7♥4♦3♦ 752	J♦6♦2♦ Q86 Q55	732 T♣6♥4♥ 985
43	52A 652 843	J33 7♦6♦5♥ 333	7♥6♥5♥ 553 654

If you hold two aces, you generally do not want an ace to flop. It will usually kill the action except in the unlikely case that someone else holds AK, AQ or AJ.[4] The only exception is when a pair also falls. Now you have aces full while an opponent may have trips, which might even become a lower full house. In general however, you would like to see no pair flop to this hand; preferably with a high card or two. However, if two of the flop cards are suited, it is not quite as good. While it is true that you will now get action from a four flush, it is also true that he will wind up beating you 35 percent of the time. (See the probability chapter.) In any case,

and

offsuited are about equal flops to two aces. You will win a little more often when 832 flops but you will not get as much action which counter balances it. On the other hand

---

[4]This is really no longer true when playing in the newer structure where pots get much bigger before the flop.

is a terrible flop to two aces — not simply because there is a good chance you are or will be beaten, but also because most players will not play a hand worse than yours when these (suited and straight) cards show on board. *This is an extremely important concept.* If you hold two kings similar considerations apply. The only difference is that the hand loses much of its value if an ace falls on the flop. (If it falls later, you have much less to worry about as I point out in the reading hands chapter.)

is a better flop to

than

for two reasons. First of all, there is less chance of someone having a six than a queen if he is playing good cards. Secondly, a hand like will give you action when A66 flops, whereas it probably will not when AQQ falls being afraid of a queen itself.

is a better flop to

than

mainly because it is much less likely that someone flopped two pair. (This of course is somewhat counterbalanced by the fact that you have a straight draw as well as two aces.)

is a great flop to AK not only because you flopped the nuts, but also because of the great possibility of having a second best hand out against you.

is not such a great flop to

even though it has probably given you the best hand. It does not figure to make you much money when it is the best hand, but it can cost you a lot when it isn't. (This is less true in the newer double blind structure.)

is in the excellent category for A♦J♦. Whenever you flop top pair, and a nut four flush, you have a great hand. Not only do you probably have the best hand right now, you are even the favorite over two smaller pair (8's and 4's in this example). You can catch an ace, jack, diamond, or *running pair* (like 66) to win. You are not even a big underdog to someone who flopped a set of trips. Even more important, is that with this flop you will get action from a smaller pair of jacks or a smaller four flush and both of these hands almost can't win! This is why I rank this flop higher than actually flopping a flush.[5] When this happens, there is very little action and even though you now have almost a sure win, you will not average winning as much money as you will with the first flop.

The A84 is not as good a flop to AJ as it is to AK because there is a greater chance that you don't have the best hand when you hold AJ (because someone else might have AK or AQ).

With the exception of the situation previously noted, where you have good reason to believe there is a high pair in the hole against you, it is always better that an overcard should fall if you flop a set of trips to your wired pair. The slight extra chance of losing is more than overcome by the increased action you can expect. Thus

or even

---

[5] Again the bigger pots before the flop in the new double blind structure makes this statement less true.

is a better flop than

if you hold two jacks in the hole.

When you don't hold a wired pair, flopping two pair is always good. It is usually the best hand and will frequently get action. The only exception is if the flop has three cards of the same suit, as well as your two pair. It is better if your two pair include the top pair. The top two pair is best since you will have your opponents very possibly "drawing dead" (plus you beat two smaller pair). If you hold second and third pair, a player holding top pair has almost a 25 percent chance to outdraw you. Even in this case however, your hand is still very good.

Flopping a full house is always very good (except when three-of-a-kind flops and you have a small wired pair).

Flopping a straight is always better than flopping a flush because the other players are more cautious when three of a suit falls than when there is a possible straight, as they should be. The reader should be able to pick out from my chart examples of the concepts I have just explained.

In general, what determines what the best flops are for any particular hole cards is simply which flops figure to earn the greatest profit in the long run. There are three criteria, properly balanced which are used to determine these results. They are:

1. What are your chances of winding up with the best hand?

2. How much action do you figure to get from second-best hands?

3. How susceptible are you to having or making the second-best hand yourself thereby costing you quite a bit of money?

Furthermore, I have made three assumptions, two of which I've already mentioned (a moderately tight game with four to six players in before the flop, and no reason to suspect a high pair against you). The third assumption is that there is not a very large amount of money in the pot before the flop. If there were, it would be more important that you flop the nuts than that you flop a hand which will get action, since the later bets lose importance in comparison to the size of the pot. With these concepts in mind, the reader should be able to understand how I arrived at my various rankings. After some study, he should be able to name good and bad flops for any starting hands.

I have purposely not mentioned what cards you would like to see on board with various hole cards from fourth street on because the betting has a lot to do with this. This will be explained further in the strategy and reading hands chapters.

For now, understanding the values of various flops to various hands is a major step in attaining full conception of this game.

Part Five

Strategy

Strategy

Introduction

There is no way to discuss every possible situation that can arise in a game of hold 'em, especially after the flop. What I have done, therefore, is break this chapter into subsections about general principles or concepts. Some of these concepts have never been discussed before in any other poker book. A few have never been discussed at all prior to this time. Many are very difficult. However, the persevering reader will find he has learned more about hold 'em and poker in general than many pros know. Eventually he can turn this knowledge into great strategic play. This section should be learned and used in conjunction with the following section on reading hands.

The only departure from the general format of this section is the first chapter on "Strategy Before the Flop." Here the number of possibilities is small enough so they can be discussed individually. A correct hold 'em strategy is unique. The reason behind this is that the best hand holds up more often than in most other poker games. If you have

and your opponent has

and the flop is

you'll win unless a queen comes (with no king). If the board pairs, this helps both of you. You still have the best hand. For this reason there are much fewer checking and calling situations than there are in other games where the pot odds frequently justify a call with the worst hand, simply in the hopes of improving to the best hand. With the exception of "come" hands, it isn't usually worth "chasing." If you can ascertain that you have the worst hand, it is usually time to fold. These factors lead to the general rule that a good player is *tight but aggressive*. He will not play that many hands, but when he does play a hand, he will try to take command. A habitual caller can't win in this game.

While the plays that I recommend have a solid theoretical basis, there are two important reasons *not* to follow them exactly. First the correct play will frequently depend on the type of game you are in, and the caliber of your opponents. I do try to indicate where an adjustment is necessary. Secondly, a true expert may have to be played differently in some situations in order to throw him off. In fact, it is rarely correct to always play the same way in a particular situation when you are usually playing with the same players. Even the best plays lose value when your opponents can pick up your pattern. Therefore, you should occasionally play a hand incorrectly (technically), in order that you don't give a hand away now and in the future.

Sometimes, more than one concept in this chapter can be applied to a particular situation, occasionally indicating opposing strategies. When this happens, the reader must balance the concepts as far as what is to be gained and lost before deciding on the right play. Only experience can teach you to do this well.

Never forget that your goal in a poker game is to win money — as much as possible (except in the case where you don't want to break up the game). Your goal is not to win pots. It is not even to have as high a winning percentage of sessions as possible. It is simply to make the most money in the long run. You must consider all the sessions as one big poker game. "Getting even," or "quitting winners," are fallacious concepts. You quit when the games becomes too tough, or you have to leave for personal reasons. How you are doing should never be a factor. This attitude is one of the most important prerequisites for a successful poker player (or any kind of gambler). It is with this attitude that this chapter was written.

Strategy Before the Flop

Whether and how you play your first two cards depends on three considerations.
1. Your position (see Part Two).
2. The events that have thus far transpired.
3. The kind of game it is.

These strategy tips are most applicable to a game with the same structure as the $10-$20 Mirage game. Remember that the man under the gun must bet $5 blind. (See Chapter One for the complete rules.)[6] It will be helpful if the reader keeps a bookmark on the *Starting Hands Chart* in Part Three while reading this section.

In early position, you should play hands in Groups 1 through 4, if no one has yet raised. In loose games you can also play hands in Group 5, as well as, any pair. In very tough games fold Group 4 hands (or worse).

If a player has already raised to your right — only play hands in Groups 1 and 2 if you are in early or middle position. Group 3 hands can be played also if the game is loose, especially as your position improves.

The proper raising hands in early position depend on whether other players have already called. If there have already been some callers in front of you, raise with all Group 1 and 2 hands. If no one has yet called, raise with AA, KK, QQ, AK, and AQ. Just call with AKs, AQs, AJs, and KQs, as you don't want to drive out players with these hands. If, however, there is a raise to your left, reraise with AKs and possibly AQs. AJs and KQs are only worth a reraise if you have many opponents. As a general rule, it is never correct to *slow-play* two wired aces. *Always* raise with this hand. (The one

---

[6]Most $10-$20 games, as do the games at The Mirage, now have both a $5 and $10 blind. When this causes a change in recommended strategy I will indicate in a footnote.

exception is in a loose game where a raise will not drive out many opponents and you can expect a raise behind you if you just call. Now you should call with two aces in early position and reraise if you can.)

If you have called in early position, and there is a raise behind you, always call as long as there has been no double raise. (If there was, you usually need a Group 1 or possibly a Group 2 hand to call.) This is assuming however, that the raise is the same amount as the original bet. If it is larger, you should fold some of the weaker hands.

Let me pause at this point to state two very important principles. The first one is that certain hands like KQ, KJ, or AJ (especially nonsuited) go down in value when an opponent raises. This is because you are in danger of making a hand only to find it is second best. While KQ is normally better than JT, I would rather have the latter hand if someone raised behind me. In fact, KJ could actually be folded if a tight player raised behind you. The reader must get a feel for his own game in order to make the best use of this concept.

The second principle is that certain hands change in value based on the number of opponents. High cards and high pairs do best against fewer opponents. Straight and/or flush cards as well as small pairs prefer many players to insure action when they hit their hand. This concept should be kept in mind when you have a close decision about playing a hand. It is the reason that it is *always correct* to play any pair when there are many callers before the flop.

In middle position you can play a few more hands — all the way to Group 6 in loose games — if there has been no raise. We have already discussed which hands can be played if there was a raise in front of you. If there was, you should reraise with AA, KK or AK and occasionally other very good hands. In loose games it is okay to just call with AK suited so as not to lose "customers."

If no one has yet called, and you are in middle position, it is now correct to raise with hands in Groups 1, 2 or 3. However, if there are already some callers, raising with a Group 3 hand may not be correct (depending on the game). This serves to illustrate two more important concepts:

1. Any hand that can call a raise cold is strong enough to raise with. This usually applies to after the flop also, and in fact, to all poker games. One frequently sees a player call a bet, not knowing the hand has been raised, and upon learning this he simply calls the full bet even though he could have pulled his original bet back and folded. Well, *he almost certainly made a mistake.* If his hand wasn't strong enough to raise with, it probably was not good enough to call a raise cold.

2. It is necessary to have a stronger hand to raise before the flop if there have been some callers in front of you than if there haven't been. In the latter case you also have some chance to steal the blinds and thus a weaker hand will suffice. This concept will be further explored in the "Semi-Bluffing" section to follow.

As you move toward the later positions you should raise with almost any hand that is normally worth a call, if no one else has yet called. Besides having a chance to steal the blinds with this play, you also gain valuable information about the hand of any opponent who calls cold behind you. If there are callers in front of you and you are in late position raise with hands in Groups 1, 2, 3 and sometimes 4. It is especially important to raise if you think that this raise will fold everyone behind you. The acquisition of last position for the succeeding rounds is worth some risks. Besides being in last position, your raise had prodded your opponent to "check to the raiser" on the flop, thus giving you the valuable privilege of seeing the fourth card for free, if you so desire. Thus, you don't need much of a hand to raise in late or last position. In fact, I raise in this spot with some hands that I *fold* in early position.

Even in later position, you must have a very good hand to call a raise cold. It can be just a trifle bit worse however than those hands necessary to call in middle positions, especially if you are in last position or think you will be in last position from now on. Also if there have already been many cold callers you can call a raise cold yourself with some of the hands that prefer play with many opponents (such as T9s or 66). Always reraise in late position with a Group 1 hand. Reraise with Group 2 and possibly even Group 3 hands if you are last and the only other player (the original raiser) is capable of pulling the aforementioned semi-blind-steal play. If you are dead last, at least call with almost anything, certainly Groups 1-6. You should call with Group 8 hands and even worse if there are many other players in.[7] If no one has called, raise the blind or blinds with anything half decent when you have the button. Strangely enough if there have been callers you need a slightly *better* hand to raise in dead-last position than in near-last position. This is because you no longer gain the extra advantage of folding players behind you by raising. You are already in last position. (Considerations like this illustrate how advantageous it is to be to the right of players who tend to show you by "tells" whether they will play or not, before it comes to them.)

If you are the live blind you should raise (when no one else has), only with extremely good hands in general. You must mix up your play to avoid being read, but in this position few hands are really worth a raise since you have to act first on every round. Against one or two aggressive opponents, almost never raise. You will be able to check raise later. If you are the blind, and there was a raise behind you, call with hands that you would have legitimately played in this position. (If the raise was to your left you can call with some weaker hands in the blind since you need not fear a reraise and you are in good position to check raise after the flop.) Beware of hands like KJ however. If there are many other players you can also call with a hand like 33 or 76s. Reraise with AA, KK, and possibly AK.

Remember that these requirements assume a fairly tough game with a small "ante." A larger "ante" naturally dictates looser starting requirements. Similarly a very easy game justifies your playing more

---

[7]This is not true for the double blind structure since a call costs too much. Stick to groups 1 thru 6 plus all pairs.

hands with the expectation of unreasonable action after the flop. Don't forget that you can occasionally deviate greatly from calling strategies to throw your opponents off, as you are not giving up that much mathematically. Any two cards can win.

Semi-Bluffing

There is an advanced technique used by expert poker players in many games which is very profitable. I call this technique *semi-bluffing.*[8]

In general, this means betting a hand (while there are cards yet to come), that is "hoping" for everyone else to fold, yet still has a chance to win even if it is called. (Blackjack players may notice the similarities between semi-bluffing and soft doubling down. If you double down with A3 against the dealer's 6 showing you are hoping he busts, but you may win even if he does not bust.)

In a situation where a pure bluff would not work often enough to be profitable, a semi-bluff may still be correct. Suppose there is one card to come, there is $60 in the pot and you assess that your hand has a 30 percent chance to wind up winning in the showdown (as in a four-flush and a little pair) and a 20 percent chance to steal the pot right here. Betting $20 in this situation is the correct play. Neglecting fifth street bets, if you both check on fourth street you will win $1,800 after one hundred identical situations. If you bet, you will win $60 twenty times, $80 twenty-four times (30 percent of the 80 times he calls), and lose $20 fifty-six times for a net profit of $2000 or $200 more than by checking. This averages out to $2 per hand, not an insignificant amount when it is accumulated at the end of many sessions.

Here then is a situation where a pure bluff would be incorrect (you're only getting 60-to-20 or 3-to-1 and you're 4-to-1 against getting away with it), as would a bet for value (you're an underdog to win), yet the combination of circumstances makes a bet mandatory.

---

[8]The subject matter of the remaining sections of this chapter are covered in more detail in my book *The Theory of Poker.*

This play comes up most frequently in hold 'em when you have flopped an inside straight draw or second or third pair with an overcard kicker. If, for instance, you hold

and the flop comes

you have a good opportunity to semi-bluff, especially if you are in early position. (Strangely enough when you are in last position it may be correct not to semi-bluff *if* you are drawing to a *cinch hand,* since by betting you now risk a check raise. By checking in last position you have guaranteed yourself a free card.) Similarly if you hold

and the flop comes

it is correct to semi-bluff with your pair of threes if you think there is any chance of winning the pot right there. A four-flush or open-end straight with one card to come, especially with a little pair, is usually a candidate for a semi-bluff. A good rule to follow is this: *If your hand is worth a call or even almost worth a call if you check, and someone else bets, then it is better to bet yourself (semi-bluff) if you have little fear of a raise and there is some chance you will win right then.*

A secondary advantage to semi-bluffing is that when you are called, and you do hit the card to make your hand, your opponent will usually misread your hand (because you bet a weak hand on the previous round), thereby winning you a larger pot than you would have otherwise expected.

A third advantage to this technique is this: If you never bluff on the flop or fourth street you are giving away too much information when you do bet. It is therefore correct to bluff occasionally in this situation. Rather than try to guess when to bluff, it is much better to *use your cards* to randomize your play. This way you are still bluffing only occasionally but you now have the extra advantage of sometimes winning even when you are "caught."

Finally, if you have made this semi-bluff play on the flop, and someone has called in front of you, you can now get a free card on fourth street if he now checks, and you didn't hit the card you were hoping for. (By betting on the flop, you may very well have caused his fourth street check.)

I understand that these concepts are not simple. However, they are extremely important so the reader should reread this section as many times as necessary to make them clear. This is especially important because many of the concepts in the succeeding sections are closely related to those mentioned here.

The Free Card
(Giving One and Getting One)

The principle mentioned in the previous section of betting when you have two ways to win (either right there or by having the best hand on the end) is valid even when your hand is not an underdog. If there is any kind of money in the pot it is usually preferable to win it immediately, if possible. If an opponent is getting 5-to-1 odds on your bet and you are only a 4-to-1 favorite, you do better, in the long run if he folds. Therefore, you should bet most of your legitimate hands to give him a chance to drop. This includes most four-flushes with two cards to come — a hand that cannot really be considered a semi-bluffing hand, but should be played similarly. An open-end straight draw should also be bet. Strangely enough these "come" hands should be bet if there is a chance everyone will fold, or if there will probably be two or more callers, since the odds are about 2-to-1 against making these hands. If you are pretty sure you will get *exactly one* call, it may not be correct to bet.

Top pair or an overpair on the flop should usually be bet if it figures to be the best hand. If someone raised behind you before the flop, resist your inclination to check to him and come right out betting. If you hold

and the flop comes

and the raiser has

if you check, you have given your opponent a precious free card to catch an ace or king to beat you. If he calls with AK in this spot you have gained a bet when he *doesn't* outdraw you. Of course, if you are fairly sure the raiser has two aces or two kings in the hole, you shouldn't bet here — but then, you also shouldn't have called his original raise with Q♠J♠. The play of automatically checking on the flop to the raiser is a major mistake. You must bet if you think you have a good chance to have the best hand. Since the pot is large, it is more important than usual that no one get a free card. You are risking a raise but the rewards (getting a player to fold who might otherwise outdraw you) justifies the risk.

By this time, the reader should realize that checking and calling is rarely correct hold 'em strategy. It is usually better to bet. When you check you probably are planning to fold or raise. Checking and calling is correct in only two situations:

1. You are slowplaying (see next section).

2. You are fairly sure your opponent has a better hand and will not fold if you bet, but the pot odds justifies your calling in the hope that you do have the best hand or that you outdraw him.

Giving a free card is so dangerous that it might be incorrect to do it even when you are a big favorite and would like some callers, yet know that everyone will fold. This occasion arises when the next card may be a miracle card that gives someone a better hand, but not likely to be a card that gives someone a second best hand. When this happens, you gain little by checking and may as well pick up the pot right there. This is especially true if you are last since you know you will not be able to check raise. *Example:* You have

and the flop comes

You should bet. You must not give single higher spades a free card. A player holding just the jack or ten of spades will probably fold here (afraid that you have a high spade), saving you the pot if a spade falls on the next card. Also, no fourth street cards will make a second best hand which will give you action. If a player holds the king or queen of spades, he will probably call, but will lose just that much more if another spade doesn't come. Actually, a player who calls a bet here with the lone queen of spades is probably making a bad play (there would have to be about $50 in the pot already to make a call correct). However, if he is only calling a *check,* you are the one making a bad play.

The general principle about free cards is this. If you check and allow someone who would have folded a bet to out-draw you, that is a mathematical catastrophe. You have cost yourself the pot. It is worth taking chances to avoid it. It is also a catastrophe (though not as bad as the previous one) if you give an opponent who would have called your bet a free card, and he now proceeds *not* to outdraw you. Here you have cost yourself a bet. When isn't it correct to bet? There are basically four occasions.

1. When you are quite sure you don't have the best hand, and equally sure you will be called when you bet.

2. When you think that someone will bet behind you if you check.

3. When your hand is so strong that there is little danger a free card will beat you, *and* a bet might drive out prospective opposition or eliminate the possibility of a check raise, on the next round. (See next section.)

4. If you have a pair of aces or kings (top pair) with a weak kicker it may be better to check on the flop to see where you stand. If you didn't have the best hand you saved yourself money. If you do, there are not that many free cards that will beat you. With less than kings, however, a check on the flop can easily result in an overcard on fourth street.

Now that you know the disadvantages of giving a free card, you can readily see the advantages of getting one. Unfortunately, there is no way to guarantee yourself a free card on the flop other than by making the unethical play of betting out of turn, withdrawing your bet and then checking when everyone else naturally checks to you.[9] However, if you raised before the flop in late position, you may

---

[9]Most modern cardrooms have rules protecting players against unethical plays such as this. For example, at The Mirage this person's money must stay in the pot.

accomplish the same end by getting everyone to check to you. You now have the option of giving yourself a free card. Take that option if you have many opponents and your hand is weak. This situation, however, is not always clear cut. If you raised as the dealer with

and only a few players called, you should bet again if the flop comes something like

and everybody checks to you. Most likely you will get called only if someone has a better hand which makes the bet appear to be a semi-bluff. However, it is also a bet with the possible best hand, not allowing hands like JT to get a free card where they can pair. By betting in this spot you will often have given yourself a free card on fourth street if you have the lesser hand, since a caller on the flop will now probably check to you, but have not given free cards to those hands worse than yours. Frequently, you will win the pot on the flop which is the best result of all.

Just as raising before the flop in late position may very well give you the option of taking a free card on the flop, this same principle also applies to the next round. For this reason, betting or raising in late position with a hand that does not seem to justify it may very well be correct. A well-known play used by experienced players is to raise in late position, on the flop, with a four-flush. The rationale is this: If the flush card comes on fourth street $10 extra is gained.

If it doesn't come, the $20 fourth street bet will be saved if everyone now checks to the raiser, as they are prone to do. While there are some flaws in this reasoning, especially if the game is tough, the play is usually correct. In fact, even if you could not get a free card on fourth street, you should raise in late position with a high four-flush or open-end straight if three people have already called, since you are getting sufficient odds on your raise. (An exception would be if a pair fell on the flop, which could lead to your losing the hand when you make your flush.)

In general, what this late position raise (or bet) on the flop is doing, is spending $10 in order to get a free $20 card on fourth street if so desired. It is similar to raising in late position before the flop with only a fairly good hand in order to try for a free flop. Both plays depend on the tendency of players to "check to the raiser." (A tendency you should fight in yourself.) Therefore, anytime you have a hand in late position that is worth a call on the flop, you should seriously consider raising.

It may be correct to raise even if you are quite sure the bettor has you beat. This happens when there is a very large pot before the flop. Let's say five players started off putting in $30 each. You are in last position with

and are sure that no one has aces or kings since you put in the last raise. The flop comes something like

If the player to your right bets (after everyone else has checked) you should *raise* even if you are quite sure he has two tens. You have to call anyway and you now do not give the other players a free card (actually a "cheap" $10 card) and instead force them to fold. Now if you do hit your ace or queen, you don't have to worry about one of the other players drawing out on *that*. It is easily worth spending $10 to avert this possibility. (You also probably gain a free card on fourth street if you don't hit your hand.) This example serves to emphasize the importance of the free-card concept.

Slowplaying
and Check Raising

The previous section indicated that it is usually correct to bet when you have a good hand. When you play this hand in some other way you are either slowplaying or sandbagging. They are not quite the same thing. Sandbagging usually means checking, hoping to raise a bettor behind you. It can also mean the much rarer play of calling a bettor to your right hoping to reraise if someone raises behind you. This second play might be called a form of slowplaying. In general however, slowplaying means playing your hand weakly, as if your hand was mediocre, for the whole round, in order to keep players in and/or set up a raise on the next round. Typical slowplays would be to check in late position when everybody else checks or just calling when someone else bets. To slowplay in early position would be to check and then just call if there is a bet.

In most cases in order for a slowplay to be correct *all* of the following must be true:

1. Your hand must be very strong.

2. You are quite sure that you will drive other players out by showing aggression, but that you have good chances of winning an ultimately larger pot if you don't.

3. The free card (or cheaper card) that you are allowing other players to get has good possibilities of making them second-best hands.

56

4. That same free card has *very little* chance of making someone a better hand.[10]

This situation will come up occasionally on the flop and therefore you should slowplay. It is very unlikely to come up on fourth street as the bets you are now losing are $20 rather than $10.

An example of a correct slowplaying situation would be where you have

and the flop comes

Even here it might be correct to play aggressively if you have many opponents and the pot was raised. In general, however, you should slow-play this hand. It is unlikely that anyone has a jack or a hand that could call you at this point. Give them another card to make aces, kings, queens, two pair or three of a kind. Though you could probably win this pot on the flop, don't try to. You figure to win a larger pot later. If someone bets, just call. If everyone checks, check along.

---

[10]With the larger pots nowadays in the double blind structure you must also not slowplay if the next card could even give someone a *draw* to beat you.

Remember that it is not correct to slowplay if the situation is not perfect. For example, if the flop is

and you have

you should not slowplay against many opponents. (It may be correct to sandbag with this hand however.) Three reasons to slow-play no longer exist in this situation. Your hand is not extremely strong. You will probably get action on the flop. There are many free cards that could kill you.

Strangely it may not be correct to slowplay when you hold

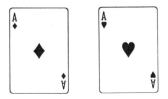

and the flop comes

of different suits albeit for different reasons. It is unlikely that a free card here will make a player who would have folded on the flop, call on fourth street. Therefore, it is better to bet and hope to catch someone with something like AQ or 66 especially if you have already been checked to. The only good reason to check here would be to *induce a bluff,* a subject on which I have a special section in this chapter.[11]

The play of just calling a bet when you are in early position to the left of the bettor, in order to hopefully reraise a raiser behind you, requires a hand almost as strong as a regular slowplaying hand. If a player to your immediate left raises and many other players call, you might even decide to raise now with a hand that you had expected to slowplay until the next round since there is so much money in the pot. Conversely, if the raiser is to your right you might decide to slowplay a hand you had originally planned to sandbag in order to avoid driving other players out.

Correct check raising situations come up much more often than slowplaying situations, as your hand does not have to be nearly as strong. It is frequently correct to check raise if:

    1. You think you have the best hand (though not a slow-playing hand) *and*

    2. You are quite sure someone will bet behind you if you check.

---

[11] Again the newer double blind structures make all of the above examples less likely to be correct due to the larger pots and the higher odds you and your opponents are getting.

This is usually all that is necessary for the situation to indicate a check raise. Thus, it is usually correct to check on the flop in early position with the probable best hand (two pair for instance) if there are many players behind you. Someone will probably bet. However, always keep in mind the risk you are taking if you check and no one else bets behind you. You are giving a free card to those who would have folded your bet and lost a bet from those who would have called. I would say you must be 90 percent sure that someone will bet behind you in order for you to check (unless your hand is super strong).

Check raising with a "come" hand is occasionally correct. The situation would be one where you think a player to your left will bet and two or more players will call by the time it comes to you. Now you are getting long enough odds to raise. Even here, you shouldn't raise if you suspect the original bettor will reraise, or if there is some chance you won't win even if you hit your hand (rarely check raise on the flop with a come hand if a pair shows). Also, you should not check raise on the come if the bettor is to your right. You don't want to drive out players behind you.[12] Normally a four-flush should be bet if it may steal the pot. Otherwise it is usually correct to just check and call.

Another aspect of check raising will be explored in the section on fifth street play.

---

[12] It is okay to raise a player to your right with a come hand if the pot is large and you have an overcard. If you hit your high pair your raise may have driven out someone who would have beaten you.

Odds and Implied Odds

At times none of the "fancier" plays mentioned in the previous sections can be used. When someone has bet and you are sure he has a better hand than you at this point, the question is simply whether to fold or to call to try to outdraw him. Experienced players know that the answer depends on your chances of making a winning hand and the odds that the pot is offering you. They know that if you are a 5-to-1 underdog, and the pot is offering you only 3-to-1, you should fold whereas if it is offering 6-to-1, you should call. In this way you will show the greatest profits in the long run. There are some considerations here, however, which even many experts overlook.

First of all, you must not confuse your chances of improving with your chances of making the best hand. If you can improve, but still lose the pot, you must lengthen your required pot odds considerably. This occasion can arise when a player may already have the hand that you are drawing to beaten. When this happens you are said to be *drawing dead*. It is also possible that a card that will improve your hand will help some other player even more. Thus, if the flop is

and you hold

you very well might not want a ten to fall. There are many different types of examples of this situation.

If the bettor is to your right, and there are other players who might raise behind you, you must once again adjust the odds considerably. If there is $100 in the pot, and the bet is $20, you appear to be getting 6-to-1 (120-to-20). However, if there is a raiser behind you and the original bettor calls, you are now getting only 4½-to-1 (180-to-40) on that round if you call the raise. If it is raised again your odds drop to 3⅔-to-1 (220-to-60). Not only that, your chances of winning, even if you hit your hand, have probably decreased with all that raising going on. This concept is extremely important yet not well known. It means that if the flop comes

and you hold

you should *fold* if you are in second position and the man to your right bets. (If there are a number of players behind you.) In this same situation you should fold

if the flop is

just to give another example. Many experts will disagree with this statement but they are *wrong* (unless the pot is very large or the game is very loose). The general principle is that you must tighten up considerably in any situation where there are players behind you who have not yet acted.

When there are two cards to come, many players make a terrible mistake in assessing their odds. They figure their chances of improving in the next two rounds and compare this to the odds they are getting on the next round only. Let's say your hand can catch five different cards to give it the "nuts." With two cards to come it is about a 4-to-1 underdog. (See the probability section). If there is $40 in the pot, a player bets $10 and everyone else folds, it seems that you are getting 5-to-1 odds and thus should call. This, however, is incorrect. The right way to determine the odds you are really getting is as follows: If you do not make your hand you will lose $30, $10 on the flop and $20 on fourth street. If you do make your hand you will win the $40 in the pot plus his $10 bet, plus hopefully a $20 fourth street bet, and $20 on fifth street — $90 altogether. Thus, you are really getting only $90-to-$30 or 3-to-1! You should fold. (It will occasionally occur that this technique will indicate a fold since it assumes you will go all the way if you play, when in fact it is correct to call on the flop only. When this happens you must compare your pot odds with your chances of making your hand assuming only one card to come. Now if you don't make your hand it might be correct to fold without seeing the last bet. This situation can occur because the fourth street bet is double the bet on the flop. One other reason to revise your estimate of the odds you are getting, from the one my method will come to, is that there is some chance your opponent will check on fourth street and you can now take a freecard.) The main thing to understand here is that your pot odds on the flop are not nearly as good as they appear to be if you intend to call on fourth street also.

It *can* happen that the odds you are getting are higher than they appear to be. I call these odds implied odds. This occurs when you are planning to take just one more turn if you don't catch your card, but can expect to win a large pot if you do. If you have

and the flop comes

it is correct to call $10 getting only 8-to-1 odds if you don't fear a raise even though it is about 11-to-1 against catching a 6. If you don't catch the 6 you fold. If you do catch it you figure to win at least $40 over and above the $80 already in there. You thus are getting *implied odds* of at least 12-to-1. This same concept is why it is usually correct to call with a small pair before the flop, hoping to flop trips, even if you don't seem to be getting the required 7½-

to-1 odds. 5-to-1 odds is usually sufficient if there is little danger of a raise. Your implied odds are at least 10-to-1 as you should win a nice pot if your card flops. (Get out if it doesn't unless you make an open-end straight.)[13]

There is a situation where you are getting what might be called reverse implied odds. This occurs where you suspect you have the best hand but your opponent will only give action if his hand is better than yours. When this happens, and he bets $10 on the flop, you know that you will probably either win only his $10 and the present pot or lose a total of $50. Your odds are once again not what they appear to be. When you see a situation like this arising, adjust accordingly.

One last situation that seems to confuse many players is this: Your opponent has bet, and you know he might be on the come but probably isn't. Be sure to adjust your pot odds to reflect the added possibility that he *makes* his hand when he is on the come. If there is one card to come, and you feel there is a 20 percent chance that the bettor is on the come, it seems that you can take 5-to-1 with a mediocre hand. However, your opponent will actually win 80 percent plus 4 percent of the time (1/5 of 20 percent) thereby making him over a 5-to-1 favorite. When there are two cards to come, it is even more dangerous to call simply because you think he has a four-flush and you can beat that (for now).

There is one reason to call if your odds don't seem to justify it. The reason is that you don't want to become known as a folder. Throw a few loose calls in once in a while so that other players will not think they can "run over you" (bluff you out easily).

---

[13]This statement is no longer always true in the double blind structure.

Bluffing

If your hand cannot possibly win in a showdown, you are making a pure bluff if you bet (as opposed to a semi-bluff). If all the cards are out, it is a simple question as to whether you should try to bluff. You should if you think you will get away with it a higher proportion of the time than the odds the pot is offering you. Thus, if there is $80 in the pot, you should make a $20 bluff if there is more than a 20 percent chance you will get away with it. Of course, accurately assessing your chances of getting away with it only comes from experience. There are some further hints on this subject in the reading hands section. If there are one or more cards to come, you can use this formula only if you intend to give up your bluff if you are called on this round. If not, adjust accordingly. (If it is fourth street with $100 in the pot, you may have to bluff twice thereby risking $40 to win $120 — 3-to-1 odds.)

When you are bluffed out yourself, it is a mathematical catastrophe. This subject is also covered in the reading hands section. For now, realize that even if your hand can only beat a bluff, you should call if your pot odds when compared to the chances he is bluffing so indicate, assuming all the cards are out. If there are more cards to come, once again adjust your odds if you plan to call all the way. (See the previous section.)

As with calling, if you are playing with the same players every day, you should occasionally bluff even if the odds don't seem to justify it. This makes it more difficult to read your hands in the future.

Inducing Bluffs

When you are up against an aggressive but tough player, it may be right to make what otherwise would be an irrational check in order to *induce a bluff*. This play can be made with a very good hand thereby making it a kind of slowplay. It can also be made with a much weaker hand. Example: You are dealt

and raise in last position. The flop comes

Everyone checks, you bet, and a tough player calls. On fourth street he checks. Check behind him! If he bets on fifth street, call him. If he checks, bet. By playing this way you save $20 if he has an eight. If he doesn't have an eight he will fold on fourth street when you bet again. Now that you checked also however, he will be induced to bluff on fifth street gaining you $20. If his hand is mediocre, he might check again, but he is now much more prone to call you on fifth street since you checked on the card before. Once again you gain $20.

Before considering a play like this it is necessary that:

    1. You are against only one opponent.

2. He is capable of bluffing but also capable of folding if you bet yourself.

3. Giving him a free card is not that dangerous if his hand is worse than yours.

Once you are capable of recognizing these situations and pulling off these plays successfully you can consider yourself a true expert.

Folding Big Pots

In most poker games it is never correct to fold when all the cards are out if the pot is very large and you have anything at all, especially against only one opponent There are times, however, in hold 'em poker where it's clear you just can't win. These situations are covered in the next chapter. For now, be aware of the fact that there are times when your opponent can't be bluffing and must beat your hand. When this happens, do not let the fact that you are getting 20-to-1 pot odds influence you. You are 1000-to-1. Save your money.

Head Up vs. Multi-Way

The general principle here is that the greater the number of opponents the less fancy you play. Slowplay less, semi-bluff less, avoid bluffing, don't induce bluffs. Realize however, that your implied odds have increased with many opponents. If you are drawing to a big hand there figures to be someone to give you action when you hit it.

Raising

There are five possible reasons to raise. They are:
1. To get more money in the pot.
2. To drive players out.
3. To bluff (or semi-bluff).
4. To get a free card.
5. To gain information.

Let us take them in order.

If a player bets somewhere to your left and gets some callers you should usually raise when it comes to you if you think you have the best hand (unless you think you should slowplay). Here you are raising simply to get more money in the pot that you expect to win. It is not very often that it is worth relinquishing this money with the best hand simply to disguise it. Just as it is usually best to bet if you like your hand, it is usually correct to raise whenever you think you have the bettor beat, even if you risk driving out players behind you.

Sometimes your raise is *designed* to drive players out. This play can only work if no one has yet called the original bettor and you are now forcing other players to call a cold raise. This play is correct even when your hand is fairly weak, possibly worse than the player who bet. However if it is the best hand or becomes the best hand, the raise has stopped the other players from drawing out on it.

Raising as a pure bluff is occasionally done in very tough games where players are capable of folding big pots without calling one last bet. I don't recommend this play especially because you are going to lose twice as much as you would in an ordinary bluff if it doesn't work. The one time where it could be used in weaker games is where you think your opponent is bluffing, but you think you can't win by calling since your hand is even worse. In other words, if you think he has a busted four-flush, you would have to raise with a busted four-flush yourself (unless you have a little pair or ace) in order to be sure to win the pot.

Raising as a semi-bluff can be a good play. Example: You have

The flop comes

Everybody checks. The next card is the

If someone bets, raise. Even if he only folds 20 percent of the time, raising in this spot is more profitable than just calling.

Raising to get a free card is a play already discussed in previous sections. This play is best when you are in late position and the bet is smaller than the bets of succeeding rounds. Any hand worth a call is conceivably worth a raise in this situation. Only the possibility of a reraise should deter you.

Some players will raise in late position or even check raise when their hand doesn't justify it because they feel they will gain information based on the reply to their raise. This play should usually be done only in head-up situations and even then it is a questionable practice. However, gaining information can be considered an extra benefit when you raise for one of the other reasons.

In fact, it is rare that a raise is done for only one of the above reasons. Frequently two or more of these reasons indicate that a raise is appropriate. Never be afraid to raise when intelligent strategic, financial, or mathematical considerations demand it.

Head-Up on Fifth Street

This subject deserves a special section because of the important concepts associated with it. (There is a mathematical technique called "Game Theory" which can be used to analyze head-up, one-bet situations but it is not really necessary for hold 'em with so many cards exposed. I only mention this so that any mathematically inclined readers will not think I overlooked it.)

We have already discussed bluffing and it will be further discussed in the next chapter. The basic principle is that you should bluff head-up on fifth street if your hand cannot win by checking, and the odds you are getting from the pot as compared to the chances your opponent will call (in your opinion) indicate a bluff will be profitable.

Assuming you have a legitimate hand, how do you play it? Let's say you are last, your opponent checks and you feel there is a 70 percent chance that you have the best hand. Should you bet? The answer is that I have not given you enough information! The question in this case is not what are your chances of having the best hand. Rather it is what are your chances of having the best hand *if you are called?* If your opponent will only call the 30 percent of the time when he has you beat, your bet was horrible. In fact, it is correct to bet on the end when you are checked to only if you think you have at least a 55% chance of winning *when you are called.* (52% is not good enough because of the possibility of a check raise.)[14]

If your opponent has come out betting, you should call behind him only if your chances of winning compare favorably with your pot odds. So for instance if you think you have a 10 percent chance of winning you need at least 9-to-1 pot odds to call. In order to raise

---

[14]Remember that we are talking about the situation where your opponent has already checked. If you are first it may be right to bet with less than a 50 percent chance as we will see shortly.

in this spot, it is usually necessary to be over a 2-to-1 favorite to have the best hand. If he calls your raise you gain $20 (but he might not call). If he reraises; you will usually have to call, and thus will probably lose $40. Therefore, you are risking $40 to win an average of less than $20. (This reasoning breaks down if you are up against a player who will reraise only if he has you beat and thus you can save $20.) Another way to decide whether to raise is to assess whether you have the best hand 55 percent of the time that *your opponent calls your raise.* If so, raise.

When you are first to act in head-up last-bet situations, it is even more complicated. You have four options (once again assuming you have a legitimate hand):

1. To bet.
2. To check with the intention of folding if your opponent bets.
3. To check with the intention of calling.
4. To check with the intention of raising.

Taking check raising first, we will assume that your hand cannot lose and that the possibility of a reraise can be neglected. Whether to check, hoping to raise, or come right out betting with this hand depends on three probabilities: the chances you will be called if you bet (assume you won't be raised); the chances your opponent will bet if you check, but will not call your raise; the chances he will bet *and* call your raise. A check raise is profitable if the second figure added to *twice* the third figure exceeds the first figure. Thus if there is a 70 percent chance you will get called if you bet, a 40 percent chance your check will elicit a bet but not a call of your raise, and a 25 percent chance you will make two bets by checking, it is better to check raise (since 40 plus twice 25 exceeds 70). If you are sure you can win one bet by betting there must be better than a 50 percent chance that your opponent will bet if you check. Even this may not be good enough unless you know he will also call your raise. Figure it out.

At this juncture let me say that I understand that it is impossible to assess your chances of having the best hand, getting called, or provoking a bet, accurately, as these figures indicate you should. However, understanding the correct theoretical plays based on accurate probability assessments can help you make the right play more often.

If you have a better chance to win a fifth street bet by checking and calling than by betting, it is better to check. This occasion arises when your opponent will bet with any of the hands that he would have called you with plus some that are worse (usually bluffs). Whenever you have bet in this situation, you have relinquished your chance to pick off a bluff. A check also eliminates the possibility of a raise.

When your opponent will call your bet more often than he will bet himself if you check, it is better to bet (even if you are an underdog when he calls), as long as you have little fear of a raise and the pot odds would have justified, or come close to justifying a call if you checked and he bet. The exact mathematical formula is too technical to show here, but just following the above rule will usually be accurate. Thus, if you are first, and you feel that your hand has only a 40 percent chance to win if your bet is called, it is still better to bet *(if you are first to act)* if, when you check and he bets, there is still some chance (say 25 percent) that you have him beat. If both players are going to put that last bet in, it is better that they do so with you having a 40 percent chance to win than a 25 percent chance. An example would be this: The cards on board are

and you hold

If you bet and get called you don't particularly like it. However, he might call you with as little as AQ. If you check, he will check AQ, but probably bet T8 and T7 as well as hands that beat yours. You must lose a bet to better hands and gain a bet from T8 or T7 no matter how you play it. By betting you also gain a bet from AQ.

The remaining situations indicate check and fold (if he bets) strategies. Once again, the exact formula is complicated, but a general rule is this: if your hand is a definite underdog *if* your bet is called it is better to check (and fold) if you feel that a bet from your opponent will indicate a hand that is almost definitely better than yours. If the cards on the board are

and you hold

you should check and fold against an opponent who will only bet a pair of queens or better even if he will call with specifically 99.

Let us summarize the options: if your hand is a cinch or a near cinch, you can either bet, or try to check and raise; if your hand is a favorite (when called), your options are to either bet or check and call. The latter strategy is used when your opponent will bet more hands than he will call with.

If your hand is an underdog when you are called (but is not a busted hand which might be profitably bluffed), you have *three options* — to bet, to check and call, or to check and fold. Once again, you should check and call if your opponent will bet more hands than he will call with, and the pot odds justify your call. If he will call with more hands than he will bet, you should bet as long as you're not that big an underdog when he calls. Check and fold if a bet is unprofitable, *and* a bet on his part will indicate an almost surely unbeatable hand.

Miscellaneous

There are four strategic plays after the flop which are rarely wrong and therefore should be mentioned apart from general concepts.

1. Play tighter after the flop if there has been *no raise before the flop*. There are more possible hands out there and the pot odds you are getting are less than if it was raised. Specifically, if the flop is something like

a high pair in the hole goes down in value when there is no raise, since there is a greater chance that someone is playing an eight.

2. If a two-card flush flops in a multi-way pot, you should play your good hands more aggressively since there is a better chance you will get called, and you don't want to give a free card. It is virtually never correct to slowplay in this situation. If your hand is mediocre but normally worth betting, it is usually correct to check if a two card flush falls. You might run into fancy raises plus you may be outdrawn, even if you do have the best hand. It is better to check here and hope everyone else does too.

3. When you have a pair in the hole, you should usually get out (if someone bets) if you don't flop trips (unless your pair is higher than

any card on board or you flop a four straight). Of course, you may bet yourself into overcards as a semi-bluff.[15]

4. If you have an inside straight draw along with two overcards on the flop you have a pretty strong hand. Thus, if you have

and the flop is

you have ten wins over a pair of nines — better than a four-flush. Play it as such.

---

[15]This statement is less true for the newer double blind structures especially if a pair comes on the flop.

Part Six

Reading Hands

Reading Hands

Introduction

Reading hands is the technique of deducing an opponent's hole cards. Obviously, your ability at reading hands has much to do with your success at poker. It is easier, as well as more important, to read hands in hold 'em than in any other game. Experts can frequently name *both* hole cards of an opponent with surprising accuracy.

There are two basic methods of reading hands. One is by noticing a player's mannerisms — the way he puts his chips in the pot, or a key pause (or lack of a pause) at a critical point in the game. This method is called picking up *tells*. The other, more reliable method, is figuring a player's hole cards by the way he plays his hand. Before explaining these techniques, I must offer a few words of caution. Do not put undue emphasis on your opinion of an opponent's hand. I know many players who *"put someone"* on a certain hand and play the rest of the hand assuming he has that hand. This is taking the methods of reading hands too far. Many times these players will go all the way with a mediocre hand against someone simply because they are sure that they are up against, let's say, a four-flush only to find they are in fact up against the three-of-a-kind that they were sure he couldn't have. Instead you must put a player on a few different possible hands with varying degrees of probability for each of these hands. I will have more on this concept later in the chapter. In any case, realize that while reading hands has a large place in the game, it can be overemphasized.

Solid strategic play of good cards remains the most important aspect of the game. Furthermore, it is important to understand that reading techniques work best against fair-to-good players. Experts are tougher, and *live ones* (suckers) are tougher still. However, "live ones" will give their money away to you if you just play solid cards.

Experts you try to avoid, but if you can't, you just tighten up more against them. With these warnings let's start reading hands.

Using Tells to Read Hands

The technique of reading hands by noting pauses or picking up tells is unreliable. The main reason for this is that an opponent can easily fake it. He may have nothing to really think about, yet he'll pause, just to throw you off. Also, even if he pauses to think, you usually can't be sure if he's thinking about folding or raising. There are, however, two examples of reading hands based on pauses that are usually accurate.

1. If a *good* player *does not pause at all* after he has bet, and has been raised but in fact calls the raise unhesitatingly, he is most likely *on the come* for a flush or straight if such a hand is possible. With almost any other hand in this situation he has to pause to consider either folding or reraising. As an example, suppose the flop is

If a player bets in this spot and then calls a raise immediately you can almost be assured that he has two hearts in the hole. With any other hand almost all players would have to think a bit about what to do. With two hearts, it is automatic. Understand, however, not to take the converse statement as true. An expert may very well hesitate in this spot with two hearts, just to throw you off. It is for this reason that the lack of hesitation can usually tell you more than the presence of it. Most players will not want to relinquish their thinking time with a difficult hand just to throw you off.

2. The only other situation where reading hands by noticing pauses is fairly reliable is when a player pauses an inordinately long time

(fifteen seconds or more) before making a call. In this case he almost always is considering folding. In my experience it is very rare to see a possible raising hand pause this long.

Reading hands by noticing mannerisms is a technique that can be used for any type of poker game. This type of "tell" will usually tell you whether the player is bluffing or not. Some players, for instance, never look at you when they're bluffing but look you right in the face when they're not. Other players do exactly the opposite. Some players may unwittingly tap their feet or shuffle their cards only when they're bluffing (or only when they're not). Some players may get very excited when they have very good hands. Of course, if you can discover any of these tells in a player, it is very advantageous. Realize however, that better players frequently fake these tells and some even *double fake* them (such as purposely getting excited with a very good hand, expecting you to disbelieve them). In any case, whether you're picking up tells or noticing styles of play of different opponents, it is important to watch all the hands, even those that you're not in.

Reading Hands by the Way a Player Plays His Hand

Let us now get to the real meat of reading hands — that is by the way a player plays his hand. By the time the hand is near completion, you can frequently name a player's exact hole cards or close to it. Remember to practice these techniques even when you are sitting out of the hand. We will start with the play before the flop. The basic questions to ask at this point are:
1. Did the player call or raise?
2. What position is he in?
3. How many other players are already in?
4. Was the pot raised before it got to him?

Just from the answer to these questions it is possible to get a good idea about what type of cards a good player is holding. (As already noted a poor player is harder to read, but this one advantage that he has, does not compensate for his overall disadvantage.) You may notice that while reading his cards based on his play before the flop you are basically assuming he is playing his cards according to the precepts I've given in the strategy chapter.

Take the situation where a player calls a raise *cold* (isn't already in for one bet). This narrows down his hand considerably. He has a very good, but not great hand. If he had a better hand he would probably reraise (almost certainly with AA or KK) and with worse he would probably fold. It is important to realize that a man who calls a raise "cold" is narrowing down his hand a lot more than the actual raiser. (This is also true for the succeeding betting rounds.) The raiser may be bluffing or pulling some kind of play. The caller isn't. Remember that many experts will often raise with mediocre hands, if no one else has called yet. In this way, if someone calls behind them, they have a much better idea of what they are up against, than if they just called and were called behind them. I haven't mentioned position or the number of players in the pot as far as reading a cold raise caller is concerned. This is because they are almost irrelevant factors in this case. An exception might be if a player is in late position, there are many other players already in for the raise, and there is little danger of a raise behind him (because the action went call, raise, call, call, call; rather than call, call, call, call, raise). In this case, the player may have a hand like 98s or 55. Another exception is that some players may not reraise with AA or KK in middle position to keep other players in. (This is a bad play on their part, however.) In any case if a player calls a raise cold, and the flop comes

you can be fairly certain that he doesn't have a pair, and can very possibly be bluffed out at this point. If the flop comes

it's a different story .

Now, let's look at reading other situations before the flop. If a man reraises a raiser, he probably has AA, KK, QQ or AK. If the original raiser was in a *steal* (late position and no one else in yet) position (we are assuming there is a "blind"), and therefore may only have been trying to steal the money in there already, the astute reraiser may be a little weaker. If a player just calls in early position, and then proceeds to reraise a raiser behind him, he probably has a pair of aces or kings.

If a good player calls in early position, you can put him on a good to very good hand. If he calls in late position his hand is probably only mediocre since he would have raised with a good hand in this position. If he calls in late or last position with many other players already in, his hand could even be worse (85s for instance), and is mediocre at best *(before the flop)*. Otherwise, he would have raised.

If a player is the first raiser, he usually has a very good hand. The two exceptions that I've already mentioned are the raiser trying to steal the pot in late position, and the expert who raises with a hand that doesn't really justify it, in order to narrow down the possible hands of those who call cold behind him (he also might win the pot right there). However, whenever a player raises when others have already called, this indicates a very good hand especially if the raiser is in early or middle position. If he has raised in late position in this situation, his hand may be a trifle worse.

Two Examples

Let us now see how to read a hand after the flop, based on an opponent's play. Once again we are assuming that he plays well (in fact that he plays like you tend to play). I will now give two examples where by reasoning properly you should be able to come up with a player's exact hole cards. (For the first example, I will go into great detail. The reader will be asked to think through the steps himself in the succeeding problems.)

Let's say the player in question called in late position with other players already in. At this point, all we really know is that he can't have that good of a hand (or he would have raised). The flop now comes

Let's say you have 77 in the hole and have therefore flopped three sevens. Now you bet, he raises, you reraise, he calls. The fourth card is the

You bet. He calls. The fifth card is the

89

You bet, He raises! What does he have? What should you do? The analysis goes like this:

The eight on the end must have helped him. With all the aggression you showed earlier, it is very unlikely he would not have raised you on the fourth card or reraised you on the flop if he already had the hand with which he is now raising. However, even so, he had a hand that was worth calling you on "fourth street" and raising you on the flop. At this point, let us look at the hands that he might raise with on the end and determine which of these hands makes sense based on his play.

1. Three queens — very unlikely — he would have raised earlier.

2. Three eights — Only a poor player would have stayed in this long with two eights (especially after you bet and reraised). Since there were many players in before the flop there is no reason for him to think that no one has a queen and that his two eights are good. (It isn't impossible however, that he has three eights since some players will simply put you on two hearts in the hole and stick with this idea all the way through.)

3. Three deuces, three threes, queens and deuces, queens and threes, queens and sevens, sevens and threes, sevens and deuces, threes and deuces, eights and deuces, eights and sevens — these hands can all be lumped together — they are all impossible. You would, of course, be happy if they weren't since you beat all of them. With some of these hands, he would have raised earlier if he were going to raise at all, and with the others, like eights and deuces, even if he would raise with the hand on the end, how could he have stayed in with it all the way? It is possible that he started

with say, Q♣2♣ (even though you don't play that) and that he wanted to make sure another pair didn't fall before raising. This is a bad play, but in any case, we have queens-up beaten.

4. A busted four flush (two hearts in the hole) — this is possible and we will return to it shortly. Certainly his third and fourth street plays make sense with two hearts. The question is, would he have the nerve to put in $40 on the end with a bust?

5. Queens and eights — This is possible but not likely. It would be aggressive, but not really wrong to raise on the flop with Q8 to knock out aces, kings, and small pairs behind him. However, once you reraise on the flop he would be very wrong to call your $20 bet on fourth street. He is only getting about 5-to-1 odds at this point, and those aren't good enough odds to try to snap off an eight on the end, which it looks like he needs. For this reason, there is only a slim possibility that he has this hand. But what about . . .

6.

in the hole — This is probably it! It gives him the same queens and eights as above but also the four-flush as a reason to play it all the way in the manner that he did. You can be fairly certain that this is his hand. (There is also a small possibility that he has 8♥3♥ in the hole. However, (a) would he have played this hand? (b) Would he have raised on the flop with this puny four flush? And (c), would he have raised on the end not being able to beat queens up? It is unlikely that the answers could be yes to all three of these questions, thereby making the possibility of this hand remote.)

There is another factor to consider here. With all the evidence pointing to his having Q♥8♥, he still would not have raised on the end if he hasn't *read you* for less. Even if he thought you had a four flush he wouldn't have raised on the end since he would gain nothing by it (you wouldn't call). He has to think you have AQ or KQ or a smaller two pair. Now, you have to think back on your play, and see if you played the hand as if you had those cards. The answer (basically), is yes. Your opponent has every reason to believe that he probably has you beaten. Therefore, he feels justified in raising with queens and eights. He feels there is a much greater chance you have one of the aforementioned hands rather than two sevens or two deuces in the hole. This is especially true, since he suspects you would have sandbagged these two hands on the flop, but you came right out betting.

Here then, is an example where you can be pretty sure of your opponent's exact two hole cards. Obviously then, you would certainly call his raise and probably reraise. Never forget, however, that you are usually laying over 2-to-1 on the end when you raise without the "nuts." (See the discussion of this concept in the strategy chapter.) So beware. Also, if you are up against a pro, there may be a problem: He would realize that you don't have AQ or Q2 because you would raise with the former, and fold with the latter (even Q2s) before the flop. He therefore would probably not raise on the end with queens and eights. A reraise on your part is no longer justified. Finally in the example given if the fourth card was 6♠, rather than 3♠, followed by that same 8♠, you must now worry about the possibility of something like

in his hand (giving him a straight). Now you can only call his raise on the end.

If the foregoing example seemed difficult, especially in the few moments available to you in the heat of battle, realize that as you gain experience it will become much easier. In order to gain this experience as quickly as possible, it is absolutely necessary that you *observe every hand* including those that you are not in. Try to name all the player's hands (or possible hands). Check yourself when they expose their hands — learn from your mistakes.

Let's try a different problem. You called in middle position with

before the flop. The player in question raised in late position. You called. The flop comes

You bet (it probably would have been better to sandbag), he raises, you reraise, he calls. The

falls next. You bet. He calls. The

falls. You bet. He raises! Using the same type of analysis as in the previous example, the reader should be able to name his hole cards. They are the

(or possibly two other high spades including the jack). With a little reflection the reader should see that this must be his hand. No other hole cards justified his playing the hand this way.

It may be right to fold in this situation even with the high pot odds you are getting. The only justification for a call in this spot is to keep players from running too many bluffs on you in the future.

The General Principle

The two examples I've given so far are rare in that you can just about call a player's exact cards. Usually you can only give probability estimates of his hand. Before giving other examples I will explain the general principle in this method of reading hands. Theoretically what we are using is a process of elimination. A player can start with any two hole cards. As he plays his hand we can narrow down these hole cards more and more. Each betting round has eliminated many of his previous possible hands. Hopefully by the end of the hand, if not before, we know what he has. In practice, however, in the heat of play we use a slightly different technique. We work backwards. At some late stage of the hand we decide which hands a player would bet this way. Then we think back to his play on previous rounds and see which of these hands made sense, based on his previous play. We eliminate the rest.

Take a hand where you have

The flop comes

Everybody checks. Next comes the

95

You still check, but the last player bets. You call. The last card is the

You check and he bets again. Now we work backwards. What cards would he bet on the end? AQ? Of course —but could he have this hand? He would not have checked this hand on the flop in last position. The same goes for any two queens or two pair. While he would have checked three queens on the flop to trap somebody, he certainly would have raised with two queens *before* the flop. It is conceivable that he has three threes or three deuces. He might not have bet that hand on the flop. What about a bluff? Could he have a hand that would justify a bet on fourth street, yet still be a bluff on fifth street? Yes, he could. He could have two diamonds or something like T9. In other words, he could have picked up a flush or straight draw on fourth street, and then busted. While it is almost impossible to read a player for a sure bluff, it is never necessary. In this case, you only need to be about 20 percent certain of it since you are getting about 4-to-1 odds. (We are assuming a $10-$20 game remember.) A call is definitely in order here. By the way, if some readers are wondering why your opponent can't have AJ in this spot, the answer is that most players won't bet this hand on the end with a queen showing. (This statement is no longer true with the bigger blind structures.)

Reasons for Reading Hands

Now let's look more closely at the reasons for reading hands. There are four:
1. To determine if a player is bluffing.
2. To determine if a player can be bluffed.
3. To determine if a player's bet can be called or raised, even if he isn't bluffing.
4. To determine if a player will call your bet with a hand that can't beat yours.

Let's take these cases in order. If your hand can only beat a bluff,[16] and the pot is offering let's say 5-to-1 odds, you must call as long as you think there is at least a 1-in-6 chance he is bluffing. While it is very hard to assess probabilities like this accurately, there are some guidelines. A player will rarely try a pure bluff from start to finish. He may try for the pot on the flop and then give up, but a bluff on the end usually means a busted come hand (as in the previous example). Suppose you have

and the flop comes

---

[16]In most cases this means having a hand all the way up to top pair with a fair kicker, since your opponent will rarely bet less.

There are many players in the pot. A player bets in early position. You call. Fourth street is the

He bets again. You call again. Fifth street is the

He bets again. You should probably fold here. He isn't bluffing. There is no possible busted come hand that couldn't beat QJ. If, however, in this same example, if the 7 and 2 were the same suit it would be correct to call most players if the third of a suit didn't fall. (By the way, most experts would raise with QJ on the flop if the 7 and 2 were suited just to avoid this sort of dilemma. By raising on the flop you have stopped him from bluffing by taking command of the hand.)

Here's another usually accurate guideline. If two suited cards come out on the flop and a third one falls and a caller now starts betting, he is almost definitely not bluffing, especially if he is betting into two or more players. This is because, if he wasn't going for a flush himself, he must suspect that another player was.

Now let's look at a situation where *you* might consider bluffing even though a bluff on the end is *rarely* a good play. It should not be tried very often especially against a weak player. But, if the pot is offering you 5-to-1 odds, and your hand has no chance of winning in a showdown, a bluff that will win better than one time in six will be profitable. There is one situation based on reading hands which calls for a bluff. That is where you are on the come and you think your opponent is on the come also. If you both busted, you can steal the pot. If however you have a small pair as well, it is not worth bluffing since you have the best hand if you have read his hand correctly. He will only call you if he has you beat and if you check, he may try to bluff you and you can pick off his bluff. An advanced concept regarding this situation is this: It is better to bluff here if you are first to act. If he was first and checked, you are very possibly wrong to read his hand for a bust since in this case he would very likely have come out bluffing himself. One more tip — almost never try to bluff out two or more players when all the cards are out. It just won't work often enough to make it profitable.

Now let's take the situation where your opponent bets and you don't think he's bluffing so you must decide whether you can beat any of his legitimate hands. Once again, all that is necessary is that your chances of winning (either because he is bluffing or because you have the better hand) are greater than the odds offered by the pot. In the previous problem, where I recommended folding QJ, you must call with AQ. There is enough chance he is betting with KQ or possibly QJ (or AQ) to justify a call. (You should probably call with even KQ.)

If a player raises you with all the cards out, it is very unlikely that you are being bluffed. It is frequently correct to fold in this spot even with all that money in there. However, if your hand can beat a hand that he would raise with, you must call. Example: If the flop was

and then

fell, and you have

and you are raised on the end, you probably have to call even though you can't beat a flush or higher straight. He would probably raise with three nines in this spot and *more importantly* he would have played two nines in the hole all the way in this hand. If, on the other hand, the flop is

and then comes

and you are raised on the end, you should consider folding two pair. He might have raised with three nines on the end but, *he can't have them.* He would not have played two nines after the flop if there was a bet.

The last problem is determining whether your legitimate hand is worth betting. It is not simply a question of whether you are the favorite to have the best hand. The question is whether you are still the favorite *if you are called.* If you are, then you should bet if he has checked to you. Even here, you should check if you are only a slight favorite if he calls, since you are subjecting yourself to a check raise. If you are first to bet, it may be correct to bet even if you are a slight underdog when he calls, since you have to call his bet anyway. A more detailed analysis of this situation was found in the strategy section. In any case, when you are deciding whether to bet on the end, it once again becomes important to read hands. You must decide which hands he may have that he will call you with, that aren't as good as yours. If you have

and the cards come out

you should probably not bet on the end. Not simply because he may have a flush, but also because if he doesn't have a flush he suspects you have one, and he will therefore often not call you with QJ or worse. (But he might bluff if you check so the right play is probably to check and call.) If, however, the last card was not a diamond, he certainly would call with any jack (hoping you have a busted four flush), and if he hasn't raised earlier, he is more likely to have a worse hand than you, rather than a better one even if he calls you. Therefore, you should now bet a KJ.

Some Final General Principles

There is no way to cover all the conceivable types of hands that may come up. However, experience along with clear thinking should get you through any situation. For instance, we really haven't discussed three-handed pots. However, as long as we are guided by the general principle that the players are playing correctly, the same techniques apply. (One important thing to remember about multi-way pots is that the players are thinking about *each other* as well as you. You must consider this when putting them on a hand.) Some final general principles:

1. Don't be afraid of cards on the end that can beat you if it is unlikely that your opponent has those cards. If the last two cards are spades, making three spades on board, don't worry about a flush if there was a *bet on the flop*. No one plays purely hoping to catch two straight spades (unless the pot is gigantic). Of course, occasionally someone falls into a *backdoor* flush, or straight by accident as in an earlier example in this book. However, that should not overly concern you. Similarly, if you have an

and a

flops, you should not be particularly worried if a queen comes on the last card since it is unlikely that it paired anyone unless they had QJ.

2. Remember to think about what your opponent thinks *you* have.

3. Know your players.

Part Seven

Probability

Probability

Introduction

With experience, most players know the approximate odds of making various hands. Only in close situations is it important to be accurate. Even here, a mistake is not tragic. However, I will mention some of the more important and interesting probabilities.

A classic mistake which many players make is miscalculating their chances when there are two cards to come. If, for instance, they have nine cards to make their hand, they know they are a 38-to-9 underdog on the next round assuming 47 unseen cards. However, they incorrectly double their wins to 18 to figure their odds for both rounds and thus arrive at 29-to-18 (38.3 percent), a figure 3.3 percent too high. I will not bother the reader with the proper technique for these problems. I have instead provided a chart for the exact probability of making your hand with two cards to come. In general there will be 47 unseen cards. I have also provided a chart assuming 45 unseen cards, as frequently comes up in head-up *no-limit insurance* situations.

To change a percentage to odds (to 1), subtract the percentage in the table from 100 and divide the result by this same percentage. *Example:* To change 27.8 percent to odds, subtract from 100 (72.2) and divide the result by 27.8 (2.597). Thus 27.8 percent is the same as 2.597-to-1.

$$2.597 = \frac{100 - 27.8}{27.8}$$

		47 Unseen Cards	45 Unseen Cards
20 Wins		67.5%	69.7%
19 Wins		65.0%	67.2%
18 Wins		62.4%	64.5%
17 Wins		59.8%	61.8%
16 Wins		57.0%	59.0%
15 Wins	(Str Flush Draw)	54.1%	56.1%
14 Wins		51.2%	53.0%
13 Wins		48.1%	49.9%
12 Wins		45.0%	46.7%
11 Wins		41.7%	43.3%
10 Wins		38.4%	39.9%
9 Wins	(Flush Draw)	35.0%	36.4%
8 Wins	(Straight Draw)	31.5%	32.7%
7 Wins		27.8%	29.0%
6 Wins		24.1%	25.2%
5 Wins		20.3%	21.2%
4 Wins	(Two Pair Draw)	16.5%	17.1%
3 Wins		12.5%	13.0%
2 Wins		8.4%	8.8%
1 Win		4.3%	4.4%

Other Important Probabilities

If you hold a wired pair, you will flop three of a kind or better 11.8 percent of the time. If you hold AK, you will flop at least one ace or king 32.4 percent of the time. If you hold two suited cards, you will flop a flush 0.8 percent, and a four flush 10.9 percent of the time. If you hold two unmatched cards you will flop a split two pair 2.02 percent of the time.

Two suited cards will make a flush about 6½ percent of the time, but this figure assumes that you will stay in with a three flush on the flop, hoping to catch two running cards.

In a ten-handed game the chance that someone holds both an ace and another card of a specified suit is about 9 percent, however, this figure decreases if you flop a four-flush in this same suit. Thus your king high flush will be beaten by an ace high flush less than 6 percent of the time (when there is a three flush on board).

An AK (or any two unmatched cards) is 2⅓ times as likely in your hand as a pair. Thus, a player who will raise with AA, KK or AK, is more likely to have specifically AK than the other two hands combined.

If you flop trips, you will wind up with a full house or better 33 percent of the time.

If you flop two pair, four straight, four flush, etc. use the chart.

Glossary of Poker Terms

Back Door Flush (or Straight): A player is said to make a back door flush when the last two cards make his hand even though he probably played on the flop for some other reason (like a pair or four straight).

Blind: The forced bet in first position before the flop used in many games. Also the man who makes this bet. Usually this is a **live blind** which means that the player in this position can raise if no one else has. (There are now often two blinds in front of the button, one small and one large.)

Button: Something that signifies the player who is in last position when there is a house dealer.

Calling Cold: Calling a bet and raise all at once as opposed to being in for the original bet and now calling a raise.

Drawing Dead: Being in a position where the cards that you are hoping to catch will still give you a second best hand.

Fifth Street: The fourth and last round of betting when the last card is dealt.

Flop: The first three cards on the table. They are turned up all at once and start the second round of betting.

Fourth Street: The fourth card on board, the third round of betting.

Nuts: A cinch hand.

Offsuit: Two different suits, used to describe the first two cards.

On The Come: A hand that is drawing to a straight or flush.

Overcard: A card on board higher than your pair.

Overpair: A wired pair higher than any card on board.

Put Him On: To guess an opponent's hand and play accordingly. To put someone on a pair of queens is to read him for a pair of queens.

Running Pair: This occurs when the last and next to last card have the same value (but different value from any of the other cards on board).

Second Pair (Third Pair): Pairing the second (third) highest card on board.

Slowplay: To play a very strong hand weakly. (See the chapter on Slowplaying and Check Raising in the Strategy Section.)

Suited: The same suit, used to describe the first two cards.

Tell: A mannerism which a player has that may give away his hand.

Top Pair: Pairing the highest card on board.

Trips: Three of a kind.

Turn: Most players are referring to fourth street when they say "the turn." Others mean the flop. Check the custom of the game.

Index